DESIGNS
BY TERRY
RICIOLI

Vintage
IMPRESSIONS
Jewelry™

Annie's
Attic®

From the Designer

Designs from the past continue to inspire today's jewelry. The romantic, vintage look has always been a favorite of mine, and it is increasingly popular today. With the vintage-style components and stones currently available in stores, it's easier than ever to create your own jewelry inspired by periods from the past, whether it's Victorian, Art Deco or a new combination like Steampunk.

Although vintage-style jewelry can be intricate and look time-consuming to create, with the use of today's components, the look doesn't have to be difficult to achieve. Chain and jewelry findings are available in antiqued metal colors of copper, brass, silver and gold. Filigree stampings and beads add a delicate, lacy look to handworked metal. Czech glass beads come in a wide assortment of wonderful finishes and shapes. Pieces like cameos, carved bone and cloisonné enamel add to the antique look.

In addition to the vintage-style components found in stores, you can easily personalize your jewelry creations to make them one-of-a-kind. Add a photo to a pendant to create your own family heirloom. Antique metals with liver of sulfur and inks; use tea to dye carved bone pieces and lace. Glue beads to filigree shapes to create elaborate focal pieces. You'll find step-by-step instructions for all of these techniques within the pages of this book.

These vintage-style jewelry designs are wearable and adaptable for any occasion, whether it's for an elegant night out or a day at the office. The Midnight Sparkle necklace, bracelet and earring set on page 17 is perfect for a special occasion, while the Asian Splendor necklace on page 30 has a more contemporary, casual look. The projects included range from quick and easy earrings, like the Tortoiseshell Dangles on page 50, to more complex designs, such as the Classical Floral Dream bracelet on page 40. So, whether you've never made a piece of jewelry before, or you've been designing for years, you're sure to find a new piece or more you'll want to create and wear.

Meet the Designer

Terry Ricioli is a freelance designer from Windsor, Calif., who has been creating original designs for publication for over 20 years. Along with beading, Terry designs in a variety of areas including plastic canvas and children's crafts. Her work has appeared in magazines, booklets, multi-author hardback books and kits. In addition to designing, she has taught crafts to children and adults in craft stores, to church groups and in the classroom. She is a Designer Member of the Craft and Hobby Association (CHA). Her hobbies include gardening, cooking and dancing. Terry and her husband, Ernie, have two children and one granddaughter.

Contents

Visual Glossary

TOOLS

Crimping Pliers are for just what their name implies—crimping! The back slot puts a seam in the middle of the crimp bead, separating the ends of the flex wire and trapping it firmly. The front slot rounds out the tube and turns it into a small, tidy bead.

Chain-Nose Pliers are the most useful tool in your entire toolbox. They are used for holding, opening and closing jump rings, and bending sharp angles.

Round-Nose Pliers are intended for turning round loops. They do not work well for holding or grasping since they tend to leave a small dent.

Wire Flush Cutters leave one flat side and one pointed side on each cut. Using flush cutters is especially important when working with heavy gauges of wire (20-gauge or smaller). One side of the cutter is flat, and the other is indented.

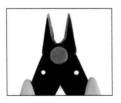

The following tools are not used in this book, but are common tools used in jewelry making.

Flat-Nose Pliers are a wire power tool. They are excellent for turning sharp corners, holding items, and for opening and closing jump rings.

Memory Wire Shears Because memory wire is harder than beading wire or craft wire, it will damage regular wire nippers or scissors. These heavy-duty shears easily cut through memory wire and leave a clean end.

Nylon-Jaw Pliers can be used to harden or straighten wire.

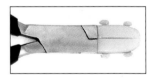

Jeweler's Hammers have fine, smooth curved heads to leave a clean impression. The round peen side works well for texturing wire and metal sheet.

MATERIALS

Eye Pins are wires with a loop on one end and a straight portion of wire where beads can be strung. Lengths and gauges vary; most earrings use 24-gauge eye pins from 1½–2½ inches.

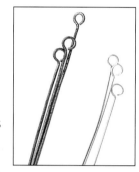

Head Pins are a piece of wire with a stop end like a fine nail head. A bead slides onto the head pin and stops on the head. Lengths and gauges vary; most earrings use 24-gauge head pins from 1½–2½ inches.

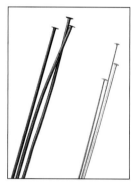

Jump Rings are one of the most versatile findings used in jewelry making. They come in all sizes, gauges and metals. They are measured by diameter (width) and gauge (weight).

Ear Wires come in many different styles. Regular fishhook styles are the most common and the easiest to make yourself. Recommended weight for ear wires is either 22- or 20-gauge.

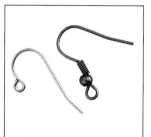

Crimp Beads and Crimp Tubes are small soft metal cylinders that can be flattened or formed around flexible beading wire to secure the ends. They are an essential component for bead-stringing projects.

Wire comes in many sizes or *gauges*. Gauge is the measured diameter of the wire. The higher the number, the thinner the wire. Wire can be tempered soft, half-hard or hard, which refers to its stiffness. Copper, silver and gold-filled are most commonly used for jewelry.

Flexible Beading Wire comes in several weights from .010–.026-inch diameters and is designed for stringing. It is available in precious metal and several colors, and it's made from 7–49 strands of steel wire, twisted and encased in a flexible plastic coating. Ends are finished with crimp beads using either crimping or chain-nose pliers.

Basics Step by Step

Creating your own jewelry is easy and only takes a few tools. Practice these techniques using less expensive metal findings. Once your finishing techniques are perfected, use real sterling silver or vermeil (real gold plating over sterling silver) to add elegance to your beadwork.

OPENING & CLOSING JUMP RINGS

Jump rings are one of the most versatile findings used in jewelry making. They come in all sizes and gauges.

Use two pairs of smooth chain-nose pliers (bent or flat-nose pliers work fine as a second set of pliers) (Photo A).

Photo A

Push ring open with right pliers while holding across the ring with left pliers. To close, hold in the same way and rock the ring back and forth until ring ends rub against each other or you hear a click. Moving the ring past the closed position and then back hardens the ring and ensures a tight closure (Photo B).

Photo B

MAKING AN EYE PIN OR ROUND LOOP

Eye pins should be made with half-hard wire to make sure they hold their shape. Wire that is 22-gauge will fit through most beads, with the exception of many semiprecious stones. Most Czech glass beads and 4mm crystals will fit on 20-gauge wire.

The section of wire used to create the eye loop depends on how big you want the loop. Here we will use a ⅜-inch section of wire for a moderate-size loop.

Flush-trim the end of the wire (Photo C).

Photo C

Photo D

Using chain-nose pliers, make a 90-degree bend ⅜ inch from end of wire (Photo D).

Using round-nose pliers, grasp the end of the wire so no wire sticks out between the pliers' blades (Photo E1).

Begin making a loop by rolling your hand away from your body. Don't try to make the

entire loop in one movement. Roll your hand a quarter turn counterclockwise (Photo E2).

Photo E1   **Photo E2**

Without removing the pliers from the loop, open the pliers' blades slightly and pivot the pliers back toward your body clockwise about a quarter turn (Photo F).

Photo F   **Photo G**

Close pliers onto the wire and roll the loop until it comes around, next to the 90-degree bend (Photo G).

Open and close eye-pin loops the same way as jump rings by pushing open front to back (Photo H).

Photo H

MAKING WIRE-WRAPPED LOOPS

Practice wire wrapping with either 22- or 24-gauge wire. Harden slightly by pulling on one end with the other end clamped in a vise, or pull one or two times through nylon-jaw pliers (Photo I).

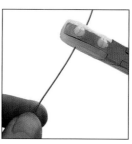

Photo I   **Photo J**

Make a 90-degree bend about 1½ inches from end of the wire using chain-nose pliers (Photo J).

Using round-nose pliers, grab wire about ⅜ inch away from the 90-degree bend and roll your hand away from yourself, toward the bend, until a loop is halfway formed (Photos K1 and K2).

Photo K1   **Photo K2**

Without removing the pliers from the forming loop, open the jaw and rotate the pliers clockwise about a quarter turn (Photo L).

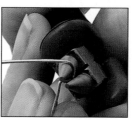

Photo L   **Photo M**

Grab the end of the wire with your left (non-dominant) hand and pull it around the rest of the way until it crosses itself and completes the loop (Photo M).

Switch to chain-nose pliers, holding across the loop. Wrap tail around wire under loop with your left hand. If you are using a heavy gauge of wire, it is often easier to use a second set of pliers to pull the tail around instead of your fingers (Photos N1 and N2).

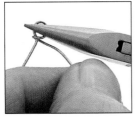
Photo N1

Photo N2

Flush-cut the wire as close to the wrap as possible. Tuck the end down if needed, using chain-nose pliers (Photos O1 and O2).

Photo O1

Photo O2

To create a wrap on the opposite end of the bead, leave a gap equal to the wrap space on the first end. Grasp to the right of the wrap space and make a 90-degree bend (Photos P1 and P2).

Photo P1

Photo P2

Repeat from Photo K1 to O2 to complete.

CRIMPING

String a crimp bead onto flexible wire. String clasp or ring, and pass tail of flexible wire back through crimp to form a loop.

Hold wires parallel and make sure crimp is positioned correctly. Using front slot on pliers, shape crimp into a small oval (Photo Q).

Photo Q

Put oval into back slot of pliers and squeeze to make fold in the center with one wire on each side of fold (Photo R).

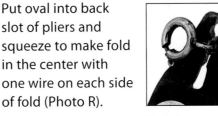
Photo R

Special Techniques

ANTIQUING COMPONENTS WITH LIVER OF SULFUR

MATERIALS

Pea-sized nugget of liver of sulfur	Sewing thread
Metal jewelry components	Plastic spoon
	Vinyl or latex gloves
1 cup of hot tap water	Protective eyewear
1 cup of cold water	Paper towels
2 glass dishes (not used for food)	Fine steel wool or silver-polishing cloth

INSTRUCTIONS

Project notes: *When using liver of sulfur, always make sure to cover your work surface, wear vinyl or latex gloves, and work in a well-ventilated area. Protective eyewear should also be worn when working with liver of sulfur. Always read and follow all manufacturer's instructions.*

Do not use glass dishes that will be used for food.

Test a jewelry component in your solution to check the strength of the solution and to see how quickly it oxidizes the item. If the oxidation is too rapid, add more hot water and stir. Different items may oxidize in different ways depending on the size and plating of the item.

1) Add a liver of sulfur nugget to glass dish filled with hot water; stir with plastic spoon to dissolve liver of sulfur (Photo 1). Add cold water to second glass dish.

Photo 1

2) String components such as beads, crimp beads, filigrees and clasps loosely on sewing thread and double-knot thread ends. Make sure there is plenty of space between items as this will allow the solution to wet all the surfaces evenly (Photo 2).

Photo 2

Stringing the items on thread allows you to dip them into the solution and remove them easily. Items that cannot be strung can be placed directly into the solution and removed using a plastic spoon (Photo 3).

Photo 3

3) Dip the strung items into the solution. Check frequently to see the color. When desired color has been achieved, place the strand into the dish of cold water to stop the oxidation process and to rinse the solution off the strand of items (Photo 4).

Photo 4

4) Remove the strand from the cold water. Cut the thread and place the items on paper towels. Pat items with paper towels to remove excess water and let them air-dry.

5) Drop loose items such as crimp covers into the liver of sulfur solution and quickly remove with a plastic spoon. Drop items into the cold water to rinse and then remove and place onto paper towels. Pat items to remove excess water and let them air-dry (Photo 5).

Photo 5

6) If items are too dark, rub lightly with steel wool to remove excess oxidation or use a silver-polishing cloth (Photo 6).

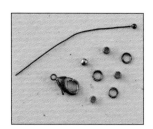

Photo 6

SHAPING METAL FILIGREE

MATERIALS

Cabochon	Round-nose pliers
Metal filigree shape	Chain-nose pliers
Fine-tip marker	Jewelry glue

INSTRUCTIONS

1) Select a filigree shape that has pointed extensions or corners that stick out beyond the cabochon that you are using. These will be shaped into the prongs that hold the cabochon (Photo 7).

Photo 7

2) Place the cabochon onto the wrong side of the filigree piece and use a fine-tip marker to mark placement of cabochon (Photo 8). These marks will not show once the filigree piece is shaped.

Photo 8

3) Bend filigree prongs or points upward with round-nose pliers or chain-nose pliers using marks as a guide (Photo 9). Check the cabochon for fit.

4) Place the cabochon inside the filigree setting. Glue it in place and let dry (Photo 10).

Photo 9

5) Continue pressing the filigree prongs around the cabochon using chain-nose pliers (Photo 11). Be careful not to mar the metal or to scratch the cabochon.

Photo 10

Photo 11

CREATING A BEADED CIRCLE

INSTRUCTIONS

Project note: *This is one way to create a cabochon or cameo setting. It works best with seed beads or round beads with a 4mm diameter or less.*

MATERIALS
Cabochon
Seed beads or small
   round beads
Size D nylon beading
   thread
Beading needle
   (optional)
Jewelry glue

1) Cut a length of nylon beading thread about 6 inches longer that the circumference of the cabochon that you are encircling with beads (Photo 12).

Photo 12

2) String the beads onto the center of the thread (Photo 13).

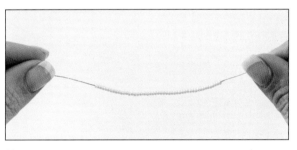

Photo 13

3) Bring the ends of the thread together and tie a single knot. Check to see if the beaded circle fits closely around the cabochon (Photo 14). Adjust the number of beads if necessary.

Photo 14

4) Tie another knot over the first. Insert the ends of the beading thread back through the beaded circle in the opposite directions until

Photo 15

Photo 16

they meet on the opposite side of the circle (Photo 15). ***Note:*** *A beading needle may be needed to help guide the thread through the circle.*

5) Tie ends again in a double knot (Photo 16). Insert the thread ends back through a few beads and trim ends.

6) Glue the cabochon or cameo to a surface such as a filigree shape, and glue the beaded circle around the cabochon (Photo 17).

Photo 17

DYEING COMPONENTS WITH ALCOHOL INK

INSTRUCTIONS

Project note: *Alcohol ink will color almost any type of item such as fabric, acrylic, glass and metals.*

MATERIALS
Jewelry components
Alcohol ink
Cotton swabs

1) Add a drop of alcohol ink onto a cotton swab and dab color onto the jewelry component (Photo 18).

Photo 18

2) Add more drops to cotton swab and dab onto component until color is as desired (Photo 19). ***Note:*** *If dyeing a large number of components, try placing components into a sandwich bag and adding several drops of ink. Squeeze bag until all items are dyed. Remove items from bag and let dry on a covered surface.*

Photo 19

TEA-DYEING

INSTRUCTIONS

Project note: *Porous materials such as bone, wood, lace, ribbon and other fabrics work best with tea-dyeing. Metal components cannot be tea-dyed.*

1) Place tea bag inside dish of warm water (Photo 20). Brew tea until dark. Remove tea bag.

2) Place items to be dyed into warm tea and let sit (Photo 21). Check to see if color is dark enough. If not, let items sit longer. Items will be lighter once they are dry.

MATERIALS
Items to be dyed
Glass bowl filled with
   warm tap water
Tea bag
Paper towels

Photo 20

Photo 21

3) Place items on paper towels and let dry (Photo 22).

Photo 22

TURNING A HEAD PIN INTO AN EAR WIRE

MATERIALS
Head pins with ball-   Round-nose pliers
   tipped heads   Chain-nose pliers
Round pen or ¼-inch–
   ⅜-inch wooden dowel

INSTRUCTIONS

1) Grasp head pin below ball-tipped head with round-nose pliers and pull head pin around pliers to create a small loop with ball-tipped head touching the wire (Photo 23).

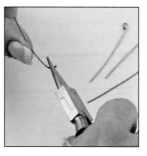

Photo 23

2) Approximately ½ inch above loop, bend the head pin over a round pen or wooden dowel in the opposite direction of the first loop (Photo 24).

Photo 24

3) With chain-nose pliers, bend the end of the pin at a slight angle (Photo 25). ***Note:*** *To add a dangle to the ear wire, open and close ear wire loop*

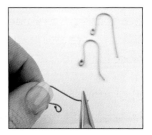

Photo 25

as you would a jump ring or use a jump ring to attach the dangle to the loop.

CREATING UV RESIN PENDANTS

MATERIALS

Pendant-shaped bezel
Desired image
Cardboard
Dark-color ink pad
UV resin
Sunlight or UV lamp

Paper towels
Toothpick or straight pin
    (optional)
Clear packaging tape
Tacky glue

INSTRUCTIONS

Project note: *The resin used on the project in this book sets up in UV light either outdoors in sunlight or indoors under a UV lamp.*

1) Determine portion of image to be used on pendant. Press pendant rim onto an ink pad. Press inked rim onto image (Photo 26). Wipe ink off pendant with a paper towel. Cut out and trim image to fit inside pendant.

Photo 26

2) Since resin may stain the image, encase the image inside packaging tape to seal it. Place the image facedown onto the sticky side of the tape and fold the tape over, covering the reverse side of the image. Use your fingers to smooth out the tape so that there are no air bubbles. Trim the tape close to the image (Photo 27).

Photo 27

3) Glue the image inside the pendant with tacky glue (Photo 28). Use your fingers to press the image into the pendant to remove any air bubbles. Let dry.

4) Place pendant on a flat surface such as a piece of thick cardboard that will fit under the UV lamp, if you are using one. If the loop on the pendant bezel does not allow it to lie flat, hang the loop over the edge of the cardboard (Photo 29).

5) Add resin to the image, letting it flow from the center. Add resin slowly, holding the bottle straight up and down; do not tip the nozzle (Photo 30).

6) If there are any air bubbles, pull them to the edge with a toothpick or pin (Photo 31).

7) To set the resin, place the cardboard with pendant into the UV lamp or place it outdoors in sunlight in a protected location free from dust (Photo 32). Allow 5–15 minutes for the resin to set up, depending on the thickness of the resin. If desired, another layer of resin can be added after the first layer dries.

Photo 28

Photo 29

Photo 30

Photo 31

Photo 32

Fanciful Butterfly

intermediate

Project notes: *Connect all components together with jump rings. String bead caps so they "cup" the rose quartz beads. Refer to photo throughout for placement.*

NECKLACE

1) Use chain-nose pliers to bend approximately ⅛ inch end of a 3-inch length of wire up against itself and press it together. This will create a head pin. Slide a glass drop bead onto head pin. Form a wrapped loop, creating a glass drop dangle.

2) On a second 3-inch length of wire, begin a wrapped loop, stopping before wrapping tail. Slide loop onto glass drop dangle; finish wrapped loop. Slide a bead cap, rose quartz bead and bead cap onto wire. Form a wrapped loop. This forms the center droplet. Set aside.

3) Form a wrapped loop at one end of a 3-inch length of wire. Slide on a bead cap, rose quartz bead and bead cap. Form a wrapped loop with remaining end, creating a rose quartz link. Repeat 11 times for a total of 12 links.

4) Repeat step 3, substituting a brass filigree bead in place of bead caps and rose quartz bead. Create a total of six filigree links.

5) Repeat step 3, substituting a glass drop bead in place of bead caps and rose quartz bead. Create a total of four glass drop links.

6) Cut chain into two ½-inch lengths, two 1¾-inch lengths and two 2-inch lengths.

7) Connect components in the following order: one half of clasp, 2-inch chain, rose quartz link, filigree link, rose quartz link, filigree link, rose quartz link, filigree link and rose quartz link.

NECKLACE MATERIALS

30mm rose quartz donut	Antique brass-plated
13 (8mm) rose quartz	wrapped toggle clasp
round beads	24 (3-inch) lengths
5 (9.5 x 6mm) brown	22-gauge gunmetal/
iris-finish Czech glass	bronze craft wire
drop beads	9 inches 4mm antique
6 (6mm) antique brass	brass-plated figure-
filigree beads	eight chain
32 x 21mm antique brass	Round-nose pliers
filigree butterfly	2 pairs of chain-nose pliers
26 (6mm) oxidized brass	Flush cutters
flower bead caps	
2 (2-to-1) antique brass	**FINISHED SIZE**
links	28 inches (including clasp)
33 (4mm) antique brass	
jump rings	

8) Connect last rose quartz link from step 7 to single-loop side of 2-to-1 brass link.

9) Connect the following components to what will be the bottom loop on double-loop side of 2-to-1 brass link: glass drop link, rose quartz link and glass drop link. Connect to top right corner of filigree butterfly.

10) Repeat steps 7–9 for opposite side of necklace, using remaining half of clasp, remaining 2-to-1 brass link and connecting chain to top left corner of filigree butterfly.

11) Slide one end of both ½-inch chains onto a jump ring. Attach jump ring to wrapped loop at top of center droplet from step 2. Attach remaining ends of chains to bottom corners of filigree butterfly (Photo 1).

12) Connect a rose quartz link to top loop on double-loop side of a 2-to-1 brass link.

13) Thread a 1¾-inch chain through rose quartz donut. Slide both ends of chain onto a jump ring and connect jump ring onto bottom loop of previous rose quartz link. ***Note:*** *Make sure chain is not twisted before connecting it to link.*

14) Repeat steps 12 and 13 for opposite side of necklace.

EARRINGS

1) Referring to step 3 of Necklace, create a rose quartz link.

2) Referring to step 1 of Necklace, create a glass drop dangle. Before finishing wrapped loop, slide wire onto bottom loop of rose quartz link; finish wrapped loop.

3) Open loop on ear wire and attach to top loop of rose quartz link.

4) Repeat steps 1–3 for second earring. ●

Sources: *Rose quartz donut, chain and wire from Shipwreck Beads; rose quartz beads, glass drop beads and jump rings from Fire Mountain Gems and Beads; filigree beads, filigree butterfly and bead caps from VintageJewelrySupplies.com; 2-to-1 links from Artbeads.com.*

EARRINGS MATERIALS	
2 (8mm) rose quartz round beads	4 (6mm) oxidized brass flower bead caps
2 (9.5 x 6mm) brown iris-finish Czech glass drop beads	2 brass ear wires
	Round-nose pliers
4 (3-inch) lengths 22-gauge gunmetal/ bronze wire	2 pairs of chain-nose pliers
	Flush cutters
	FINISHED SIZE
	2 inches long

Photo 1

Midnight Sparkle

easy

Project notes: *Use jump rings to connect components. A filigree bead is used as a connector in this variation on a Y-necklace.*

NECKLACE

1) Slide a filigree bead onto an eye pin and form a simple loop above bead, creating a filigree link. Repeat six times for a total of seven filigree links.

2) In the same manner, create 17 oval links using faceted glass ovals.

3) Create a bicone link by sliding a black glass bicone, black diamond bicone and black glass bicone onto an eye pin, forming a simple loop above last bicone. Repeat seven times for a total of eight bicone links.

4) Referring to photo for placement, slide a jump ring through center bottom of one filigree link. Before closing jump ring, slide an oval link onto jump ring; close jump ring. Use a jump ring to attach remaining loop of oval link to pendant loop; close jump ring.

NECKLACE MATERIALS

Black enamel filigree scallop pendant

7 (12mm) gunmetal filigree round beads

17 (9 x 6mm) black faceted glass oval beads

Bicone crystals:
  16 (4mm) black glass,
  8 (5mm) black diamond
  CRYSTALLIZED™ - Swarovski Elements

32 (2-inch) 20-gauge gunmetal eye pins

34 (6mm) gunmetal-plated jump rings (opened)

Gunmetal hook-and-eye clasp

Round-nose pliers

2 pairs of chain-nose pliers

Flush cutters

FINISHED SIZE

33 inches (including clasp)

5) Starting on one loop of filigree link from step 4, connect the following: oval link, bicone link, oval link and a filigree link. Repeat sequence twice.

6) In the same manner, connect the following to complete one side of necklace: oval link, bicone link, oval link and one half of clasp.

7) Repeat steps 5 and 6 for remaining half of necklace.

EARRINGS

1) Slide a filigree bead onto an eye pin and form a simple loop above bead creating a filigree link.

2) Slide a faceted glass oval, black diamond bicone and black glass bicone onto a head pin. Form a simple loop above last bead, creating a dangle.

3) Open loop on dangle and attach it to loop on filigree link; close loop.

4) Open remaining loop on filigree link and slide it onto ear wire; close loop.

5) Repeat steps 1–4 for second earring.

EARRINGS MATERIALS
2 (12mm) gunmetal filigree round beads
2 (9 x 6mm) black faceted glass oval beads
Bicone crystals:
 2 (4mm) black glass,
 2 (5mm) black diamond
CRYSTALLIZED™ - Swarovski Elements

2 (2-inch) 20-gauge gunmetal head pins
2 (2-inch) 20-gauge gunmetal eye pins
2 gunmetal ear wires
Round-nose pliers
Flush cutters

FINISHED SIZE
2 inches long

BRACELET MATERIALS
5 (12mm) gunmetal filigree round beads
4 (9 x 6mm) black faceted glass oval beads
9 (2-inch) 20-gauge gunmetal eye pins
10 (6mm) gunmetal-plated jump rings (opened)

10mm gunmetal-plated pewter toggle clasp
Round-nose pliers
2 pairs of chain-nose pliers
Flush cutters

FINISHED SIZE
8¼ inches (including clasp)

BRACELET

1) Slide a filigree bead onto an eye pin; form a simple loop above bead, creating a filigree link. Repeat four times for a total of five filigree links.

2) In the same manner, create four oval links using eye pins and faceted glass ovals.

3) Slide one half of clasp and a filigree link onto a jump ring; close jump ring. Slide remaining loop of filigree link and an oval link onto an open jump ring; close jump ring. Connect remaining links together in this manner as shown.

4) Slide remaining loop of last filigree link and remaining half of clasp onto a jump ring; close jump ring. ●

Sources: *Jolee's™ filigree pendant from EK Success; Beyond Beautiful filigree round beads, faceted glass ovals and glass bicones from Cousin Corp. of America; CRYSTALLIZED™ - Swarovski Elements bicone crystals, eye pins and jump rings from Artbeads.com.*

Sapphire Elegance

intermediate

Project notes: *Oxidation of metals occurs naturally over time with exposure to air. You can speed up the aging process with liver of sulfur, which adds a dark patina to silver. Dip all the silver findings into the liver of sulfur solution following the Antiquing Components With Liver of Sulfur instructions on page 9.*

Button pearls have a rounded side and a flat side. Place flat sides against heishi spacers.

NECKLACE

1) Slide a jump ring through top loop of chandelier earring finding and an end loop on one scroll connector; close jump ring. Repeat to attach remaining connector to earring finding.

2) Slide an 8mm faceted round crystal, pearl, heishi spacer, pearl and a 6mm bicone crystal onto a head pin; form a wrapped loop above beads. Repeat twice for a total of three dangles. Using jump rings, attach dangles to bottom loops of earring finding.

3) Slide a 6mm bicone crystal, pearl, heishi spacer, pearl and a 4mm bicone crystal onto a head pin; form a wrapped loop above beads. Repeat three times for a total of four dangles. Referring to photo and using jump rings, attach a dangle to center loop and end loop on a scroll connector. Repeat to attach remaining two dangles to second connector.

NECKLACE MATERIALS

Dark sapphire crystals:
- 24 (4mm) bicone,
- 19 (6mm) bicone,
- 3 (8mm) faceted round
- 38 (5–6mm) gray button pearls
- 19 (4mm) antique silver twist heishi spacers
- 42 (3mm) silver-plated round beads
- 7 (2-inch) silver-plated 24-gauge ball-tipped head pins
- 9 (4mm) silver-plated jump rings (opened)
- 4 (1.3mm) silver crimp beads
- 4 silver crimp covers
- Sterling silver Bali chandelier earring finding (#99198a)

- 2 sterling silver double scroll connectors (#91021)
- Sterling silver hook-and-eye clasp with soldered rings
- 2 (11-inch) lengths .018-inch-diameter nylon-coated flexible beading wire
- Liver of sulfur
- Fine steel wool
- Round-nose pliers
- Chain-nose pliers
- Crimping pliers
- Flush cutters

FINISHED SIZE

19 inches (including clasp)

4) String a crimp bead onto one 11-inch length of beading wire ½ inch from end. Pass wire through loop on one scroll connector and back through crimp bead. Using crimping pliers, crimp the crimp bead. Use crimping pliers to close a crimp cover over crimp bead. Trim wire tail as needed.

5) String a 6mm bicone crystal, 3mm round bead, pearl, heishi spacer, pearl and a 3mm round bead onto beading wire. Repeat five more times.

6) String a 4mm bicone crystal and a 3mm round bead onto beading wire; repeat eight more times.

7) String a 4mm bicone crystal and a crimp bead. Pass wire through soldered ring on hook half of clasp. Pass wire back through crimp bead. Crimp in the same manner as before, leaving some slack between crimp bead and clasp; the crimp cover will take up this space. In the same manner as before, cover crimp bead with a crimp cover. *Note: Be careful when crimping next to a crystal as crimping pliers can break crystals.*

8) Repeat steps 4–7 on opposite side of necklace using remaining half of clasp.

EARRINGS

1) Slide a 6mm bicone crystal, pearl, heishi spacer, pearl and a 4mm bicone crystal onto a head pin. Form a wrapped loop above beads, creating a dangle. Repeat once.

2) Slide an 8mm faceted round crystal, pearl, heishi spacer, pearl and a 6mm bicone crystal onto a head pin. Form a wrapped loop above beads, creating a dangle.

3) Referring to photo, use jump rings to connect dangles to bottom loops of a chandelier earring finding.

4) Use flush cutters to cut ball-tipped head off of a head pin. Form a wrapped loop on one end of head pin. Slide on an 8mm faceted round crystal. Form a wrapped loop above crystal, sliding loop onto loop on ear wire before wrapping. Use a jump ring to attach opposite end of link to top loop on chandelier earring finding.

5) Repeat steps 1–4 for second earring. ●

Sources: *Crystals from Cousin Corp. of America; pearls and liver of sulfur from Fire Mountain Gems and Beads; heishi spacers and head pins from Artbeads.com; silver-plated round beads from Jo-Ann Stores Inc.; Bali chandelier earring findings, connectors and ear wires from Imagine It Inc.; beading wire, crimp beads and crimp covers from Beadalon.*

EARRINGS MATERIALS

Dark sapphire crystals:
 4 (4mm) bicone,
 6 (6mm) bicone,
 4 (8mm) faceted round
12 (5–6mm) gray button pearls
6 (4mm) antique silver twist heishi spacers
8 (2-inch) silver-plated 24-gauge ball-tipped head pins
8 (4mm) silver-plated jump rings (opened)

2 sterling silver Bali chandelier earring findings (#99198a)
2 silver ear wires
Liver of sulfur
Steel wool
Round-nose pliers
Chain-nose pliers
Flush cutters

FINISHED SIZE
3¾ inches long

Graceful Garnet

intermediate

Project note: *The chain used on this project consists of one long oval link alternating with three smaller oval links. Separate chain by opening long oval links in the same manner as a jump ring. Lengths of chain for this set begin and end with three small links.*

NECKLACE MATERIALS
Brass Crown Pendant
    Set: 44 x 32mm brass
    diamond-shaped
    filigree pendant
Transparent dark garnet
    fire-polished glass
    beads: 7 (4mm) round,
    23 (5x7mm) faceted
    drop
8 (2mm) antique brass
    metal round beads
Bead caps: 23 (4mm) brass
    oxide pewter scalloped,
    1 (9mm) brass 4-petal
    flower
Bronze jump rings
    (opened): 27 (4mm),
    6 (6mm)

24 (2-inch) antique gold-
    plated brass 22-gauge
    head pins
Brass oxide classic toggle
    clasp set
Antique gold chain with
    long and short ovals:
    4 (1¾-inch) lengths,
    4 (2¼-inch) lengths,
    2 (3³⁄₁₆-inch) lengths
Toothpick
Round-nose pliers
2 pairs of chain-nose pliers
Flush cutters
Jewelry glue

FINISHED SIZE
16½ inches (including clasp)

NECKLACE

1) Slide a brass round bead and 9mm bead cap (cup up) onto a head pin. Slide pin through center hole of filigree pendant positioning bead cap on front of pendant. Trim head pin to ⅜ inch on back of pendant and form a simple loop. Press loop down against back of pendant with chain-nose pliers. Check to see that bead cap is straight on front of pendant and use a toothpick to add a dot of glue to loop and back of bead cap to hold bead cap in place. Let glue dry (Photo 1).

Photo 1

2) Slide a faceted drop bead and scalloped bead cap onto a head pin. Form a wrapped loop, creating a drop dangle. Repeat 15 times for a total of 16 drop dangles.

3) In the same manner, slide a faceted drop bead, scalloped bead cap, 4mm round bead and brass round bead onto a head pin. Form a wrapped loop, creating a round/drop dangle. Repeat six times for a total of seven round/drop dangles.

4) Slide a 4mm jump ring through hole on one side of filigree pendant. Close jump ring.

5) Slide a 6mm jump ring through 4mm jump ring from step 4. Slide one end of a 2¼-inch chain and one end of a 1¾-inch chain onto the 6mm jump ring; close jump ring.

6) Slide remaining ends of chains from step 5 onto another 6mm jump ring, making sure chains are not twisted and that longer chain hangs below shorter chain. Slide on one end of another 2¼-inch chain and one end of another 1¾-inch chain; close jump ring.

7) Slide remaining ends of chains from step 6 onto a 6mm jump ring. Slide one end of a 3³⁄₁₆-inch chain onto jump ring; close jump ring.

8) Slide remaining end of 3³⁄₁₆-inch chain onto a 4mm jump ring. Slide one half of clasp onto jump ring; close jump ring.

9) Repeat steps 4–8 for opposite side of necklace using remaining half of clasp.

10) Referring to photo for placement and using 4mm jump rings, connect drop dangles onto long links of 2¼-inch chains (Photo 2).
Note: Four drop dangles will be attached to each 2¼-inch chain.

Photo 2

11) In the same manner, using 4mm jump rings, connect round/drop dangles to bottom edge of filigree pendant as shown in Photo 3.

Photo 3

Garnet was a popular stone for jewelry in Victorian times. In this necklace, fire-polished glass beads stand in for the dark red garnets once mined in Bohemia. Fire-polished glass is a pressed glass made in metal molds. Fire-polishing after molding smoothes the glass and removes any remnants of the seam.

BRACELET

Project note: *Wear this bracelet with each strand apart or twist the strands together two or three times before clasping for a different look. Twisting the strands together will shorten the bracelet.*

1) Slide a garnet bead onto an eye pin. Form a simple loop, creating a link. Repeat 27 times for a total of 28 links.

2) Use a 4mm jump ring to connect two garnet links together. Continue using 4mm jump rings to connect a total of 14 garnet links together, creating a garnet chain.

3) Repeat step 2 to create a second garnet chain.

4) Slide the following onto a 6mm jump ring in desired order: one 6⅞-inch chain, one garnet chain, one 6⅞-inch chain, one garnet chain and one 6⅞-inch chain; close jump ring. Slide opposite ends of all chains onto a second 6mm jump ring in the same order as you attached the first ends.

5) Slide a 6mm jump ring through a jump ring from step 4. Slide on one half of clasp; close jump ring.

6) Repeat step 5 on opposite end of bracelet using remaining half of clasp.

BRACELET MATERIALS
28 (4mm) transparent dark garnet fire-polished glass beads
Bronze jump rings (opened): 26 (4mm), 4 (6mm)
28 (2-inch) antique gold-plated brass 22-gauge eye pins
Antique brass-plated wrapped toggle clasp
3 (6⅞-inch) lengths antique gold chain with long and short ovals (each length should begin and end with two short ovals)
Round-nose pliers
2 pairs chain-nose pliers
Flush cutters

FINISHED SIZE
8 inches (including clasp)

EARRINGS

1) Slide faceted drop bead, bead cap, 4mm round bead and brass bead onto a head pin. Form a wrapped loop, creating a round/drop dangle.

2) Form a wrapped loop on one 3-inch length of wire 1 inch from end. Slide on a 6mm round bead and form a wrapped loop, creating a bead link.

3) Slide a jump ring through top hole of triangular filigree. Slide on bead link; close jump ring.

4) Open loop on an ear wire; slide onto top loop of bead link. Close loop.

5) Slide a jump ring through each hole on bottom edge of triangular filigree; close jump rings.

6) Slide a jump ring through end of a length of chain. Slide the jump ring onto one of the outer jump rings from step 5; close jump ring. Repeat to attach a second chain to opposite side of filigree.

7) Slide remaining end of one chain from step 6, a round/drop dangle and remaining end of other chain from step 6 onto a jump ring. Slide jump ring onto jump ring attached to center hole of filigree triangle; close jump ring.

8) Repeat steps 1–7 for second earring. ●

Sources: *Brass Crown Pendant Set (#56-12297) and brass bead caps (#56-10072) from Laliberi; fire-polished beads from Shipwreck Beads; brass oxide pewter bead caps and toggle clasps from Artbeads.com; jump rings from Cousin Corp. of America; antique brass-plated metal beads from MK Beads; head pins and eye pins from Fire Mountain Gems and Beads; craft wire, chain and E-6000® jewelry glue from Michaels Stores Inc.*

EARRINGS MATERIALS

Brass Crown Pendant Set:
  2 swirl crown triangular filigrees
Transparent dark garnet fire-polished glass beads: 2 (4mm) round, 2 (6mm) round, 2 (5 x 7mm) faceted drop
2 (4mm) brass oxide pewter scalloped bead caps
2 (2mm) antique brass metal beads
14 (4mm) bronze jump rings (opened)

2 (2-inch) antique gold-plated brass 22-gauge head pins
2 (3-inch) lengths gunmetal/bronze 22-gauge craft wire
4 (1¼-inch) lengths antique gold chain with long and short ovals
2 antique brass ear wires
Round-nose pliers
2 pairs of chain-nose pliers
Flush cutters

FINISHED SIZE
3 inches long

Emerald Glamour

easy

1) Referring to Shaping Metal Filigree technique on page 10, shape Sea Petals filigree piece around oval cabochon.

2) Using jewelry glue, attach wrapped oval cabochon to center of Garden Trellis filigree piece; let dry completely.

3) Referring to photo, slide jump ring onto large loop at one end of a 10-inch length of chain and through an opening on top corner of Garden Trellis filigree; close jump ring. Repeat on opposite top corner of filigree piece.

4) Slide jump ring onto large loop at end of a 1¼-inch length of chain and through an opening on bottom corner of Garden Trellis filigree piece; close jump ring. Repeat on opposite bottom corner of filigree piece.

5) Slide a glass drop bead and a bead cap onto a head pin. Form a simple loop above bead cap, creating a dangle. Repeat twice for a total of three dangles.

6) Slide a jump ring through remaining end of one 1¼-inch length of chain. Slide a dangle onto the same jump ring followed by remaining end of other 1¼-inch length of chain; close jump ring.

7) Slide a jump ring onto a dangle and then through one jump ring attached to bottom corner of filigree piece; close jump ring. Repeat on remaining side of filigree piece.

8) Slide a jump ring onto remaining end of a 10-inch length of chain and one half of clasp; close jump ring. Repeat on opposite side of necklace using remaining half of clasp. ●

Sources: *Filigree components, jump rings, head pins, ladder chain and clasp from Vintaj Natural Brass Co.; oval cabochon from Artbeads.com; glass drop beads from Fire Mountain Gems and Beads.*

MATERIALS

13 x 18mm emerald foiled glass oval cabochon
3 (17 x 11mm) transparent honey glass drop beads
Filigree components:
  1 (40mm) copper Garden Trellis, 1 (26mm) natural brass Sea Petals Fastenables™
3 (7mm) natural brass filigree bead caps
9 (5.25mm) brass jump rings (opened)

3 (2-inch) 20-gauge brass head pins
21 x 6mm brass hook-and-eye clasp
Brass ladder chain:
  2 (10-inch) lengths,
  2 (1¼-inch) lengths
Round-nose pliers
2 pairs of chain-nose pliers
Flush cutters
Jewelry glue

FINISHED SIZE
28 inches (including clasp)

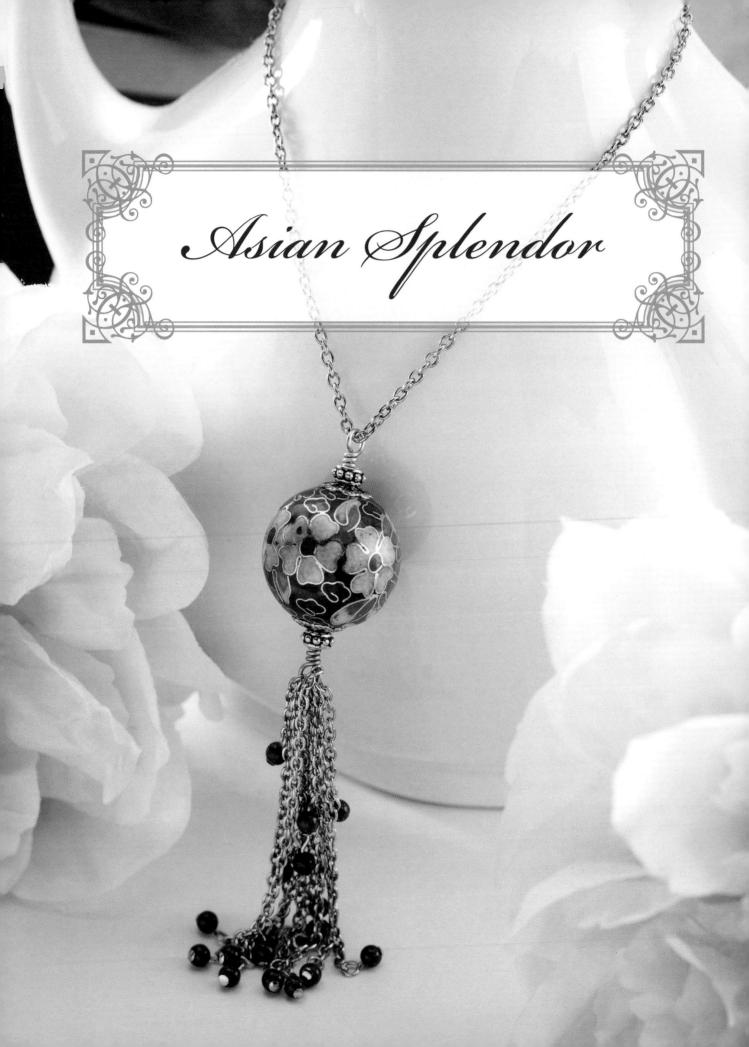

Asian Splendor

easy

Project note: *String bead caps so they "cup" the cloisonné bead.*

1) Referring to Dyeing Components With Alcohol Ink technique on pages 11 and 12, dye bead caps, wire, chain and head pins with golden brown ink. Let dry and repeat until desired color is achieved, keeping in mind uneven color adds to the vintage look.

2) Working in middle of round-nose pliers, form a large wrapped loop 2 inches from one end of wire. Slide on a beaded spacer, bead cap, cloisonné bead, bead cap and beaded spacer. Start to make a large wrapped loop at right angle to the first loop, but do not wrap it.

3) Cut chain into nine 2½-inch lengths and one 26-inch length. Slide short lengths of chain onto unfinished wrapped loop; finish wrapping loop. Use chain-nose pliers to press end of wire underneath spacer.

4) Slide a lapis bead onto a head pin. Form a simple loop, creating a dangle. Repeat 17 times for a total of 18 lapis dangles. Open loops and attach dangles to ends of 2½-inch chains. Attach remaining dangles as desired onto 2½-inch chains.

5) Slide remaining length of chain through top loop of cloisonné bead link. Use jump rings to attach each half of clasp to ends of long chain. ●

Sources: *Cloisonné bead from Shipwreck Beads; lapis beads and bead caps from Michaels Stores Inc.; beaded spacers from Artbeads. com; chain from Blue Moon Beads; wire and jump rings from Darice Inc.; head pins from Fire Mountain Gems and Beads; alcohol ink from Ranger Industries Inc.*

MATERIALS	
20mm blue round cloisonné bead	50 inches gold fine cable chain
18 (4mm) synthetic lapis round beads	7 inches (20-gauge) gold-color wire
2 (7mm) antique gold beaded spacers	Golden brown alcohol ink
2 (9mm) gold filigree bead caps	Cotton swab
	Clear sandwich bag
18 (1-inch) gold-plated head pins	Round-nose pliers
	2 pairs of chain-nose pliers
2 (4mm) gold-plated jump rings (opened)	Flush cutters
Antique gold rope toggle clasp	**FINISHED SIZE**
	28 inches (including clasp)

Timeless Treasures

easy

Project note: *To personalize this necklace, add your favorite trinkets and charms instead of the materials listed.*

1) Use blade of a kitchen knife to carefully remove back of watch frame. Press watch back rim into ink pad and press onto cardstock. Wipe ink off watch back rim. Cut out cardstock along outline. Trim if necessary to fit into watch frame back.

2) Referring to Tea-Dyeing technique on page 12, dye fabrics, lace scraps and buttons as desired. Let dry. Iron fabrics as needed.

3) Rub needle threader into black ink. Rub off excess ink with paper towel.

4) Referring to Dyeing Components With Alcohol Ink technique on pages 11 and 12, add color to various components with brown ink as desired for an aged effect.

5) Adhere fabric to cardstock circle. Trim excess fabric along edges. Adhere fabric/cardstock circle inside of watch back.

6) Position and adhere desired fabrics, lace scraps, needle threader, buttons and components to fabric-covered watch back. *Note: If fabric scraps extend past edges of watch frame, trim edges as needed to fit.*

7) Snap back into watch front.

8) Slide chain through watch bail and connect ends with ball chain connector.

9) Use jump rings to attach shank buttons or charms onto watch bail and tie lace onto bail as shown. ●

Sources: *Tim Holtz® idea-ology® pocket watch frame and alcohol ink from Ranger Industries Inc.; tacky glue from iLoveToCreate™.*

MATERIALS

Pocket watch frame
3-inch square of cardstock
3-inch square of cotton print fabric
Scraps of lace and fabric
Vintage buttons, snaps and studs
Mini safety pins
2 buttons with attached shanks or charms
Metal needle threader
2 (6mm) antique gold-plated jump rings (opened)

36 inches antique nickel ball chain with connector
Black ink pad
Brown alcohol ink
Cotton swab
Paper towels
Tea bag
2 pairs of chain-nose pliers
Tacky glue

FINISHED SIZE
40 inches

Cameo Beauty

intermediate

Project note: *Infinity chain is composed of an oval link and an a link shaped like an infinity symbol (∞). Cut lengths so each end is an oval link. Use 6mm jump rings unless instructed otherwise.*

1) Using flush cutters, remove loop from filigree pendant. Smooth rough edges with metal file. Referring to photo, adhere cameo to filigree pendant using jewelry glue. Let dry completely.

2) Referring to Creating a Beaded Circle technique on page 11, create a beaded circle with approximately 19 fire-polished glass beads. **Note:** *Make sure beaded circle will fit around cameo before finishing circle.* Glue circle around cameo.

3) In the same manner as for cameo, adhere resin rose cabochons to edges of filigree pendant.

4) Slide a 4mm glass bead onto a head pin. Form a simple loop, creating a dangle. Repeat three times for a total of four dangles. Slide 16 x 8mm glass bead onto a head pin. Form a simple loop, creating a dangle.

5) Slide a jump ring through large open space on bottom left edge of filigree pendant as shown; slide one 1-inch length of chain onto jump ring. Close ring. Repeat for opposite side of pendant.

6) Slide remaining ends of 1-inch chains onto another jump ring. Before closing ring, slide on beaded dangles from step 4. Close ring.

7) Slide a jump ring through large open space on top left edge of filigree pendant as shown. Slide one end of a 12⅛-inch length of chain onto jump ring. Close ring. Repeat for opposite side of pendant.

8) Use a jump ring to attach one half of clasp to end of one 12⅛-inch chain. Repeat to attach 8mm jump ring to remaining end of necklace. ●

Sources: *Cameo, rose cabochons, beading thread and chain from Artbeads.com; fire-polished glass beads from A Grain of Sand; twisted pressed-glass bead from Fire Mountain Gems and Beads; filigree pendant from Making Memories; head pins from VintageJewelrySupplies.com.*

MATERIALS

18 x 25mm carnelian and ivory resin cameo
23–25 (4mm) red/white fire-polished glass beads
16 x 8mm peach/gold twisted pressed-glass bead
6.5mm resin rose cabochons: 2 coral, 4 pink
50 x 36mm antique gold metal filigree pendant
Antique brass-plated jump rings (opened): 7 (6mm), 1 (8mm)
5 (1½-inch) oxidized brass ball-tipped head pins

14mm brass-finish lobster-claw clasp
10 inches brown nylon beading thread
Antique brass-plated 1+1 Infinity Link chain: 2 (1-inch) lengths, 2 (12⅛-inch) lengths
Beading needle (optional)
Metal file
Round-nose pliers
2 pairs of chain-nose pliers
Flush cutters
Jewelry glue

FINISHED SIZE

31 inches (including clasp)

Enchanting Garden

Floral images are a common element in Victorian-style jewelry designs and were especially popular during the late Georgian period.

easy

1) Referring to Creating UV Resin Pendants technique on page 13, create a pendant using oval bezel and botanical flower print.

2) Thread ribbon through pendant loop. To wear, tie ends in a bow or knot. ●

Sources: *ATC Botanicals Paper Pad from Leisure Arts; ribbon from Artbeads.com; UV lamp and Magic-Gloss® UV resin from JHB International Inc.*

MATERIALS

Large silver-plated oval
    bezel pendant
Botanical flower print
    sized to fit inside
    pendant
Black ink pad
33 inches green silk ribbon
UV lamp or sunlight
Cardboard

Paper towels
Toothpick or straight pin
    (optional)
Clear packaging tape
UV resin
Tacky glue

FINISHED SIZE

28 inches

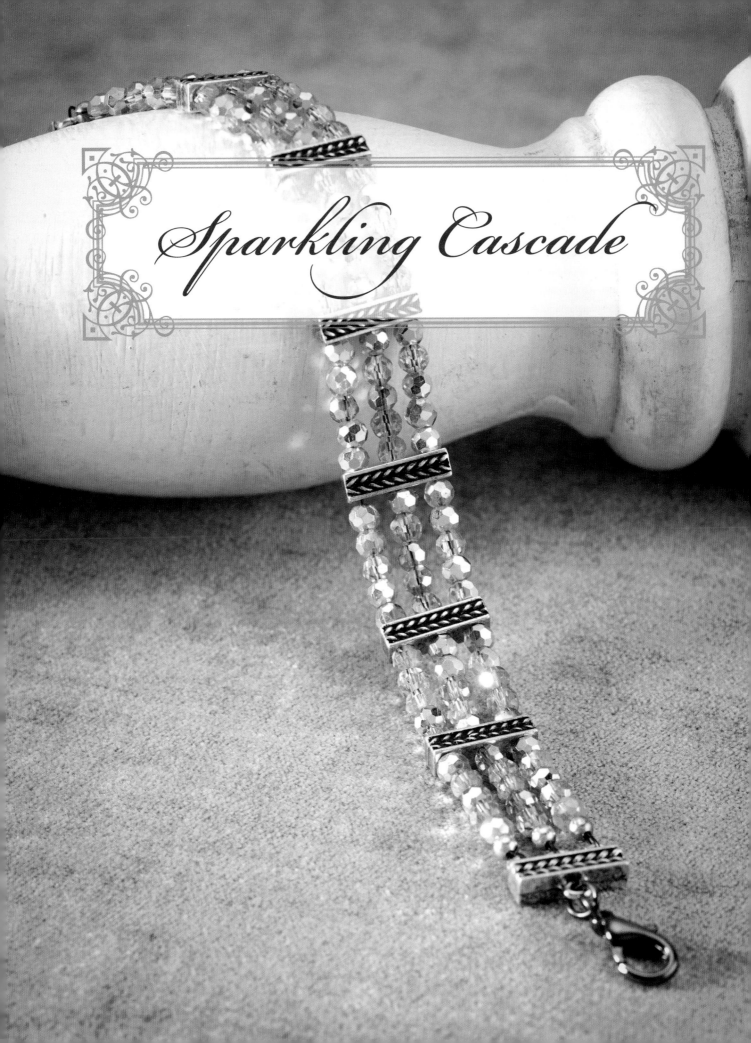

Sparkling Cascade

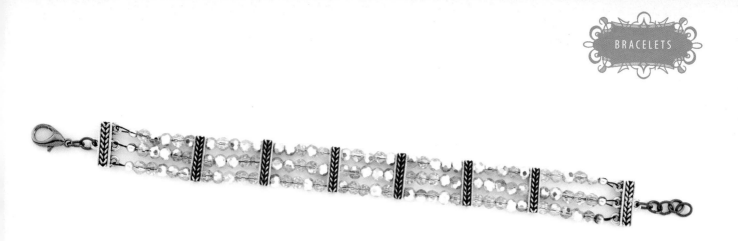

easy

Project notes: *If bracelet length is too long, reduce number of beads used at each end of bracelet pattern. Use tape to secure ends of wire not being strung.*

1) String a crimp bead onto one 10-inch length of beading wire ½ inch from end. Slide beading wire through a loop on 3-loop side of a 3-to-1 link. Thread wire back through crimp bead and use crimping pliers to crimp the bead. Repeat to attach remaining lengths of wire to remaining holes on 3-loop side of 3-to-1 link, keeping loops consistent.

2) If desired, cover crimp beads with crimp covers; close covers over crimp beads using crimping pliers.

3) Slide five 4mm beads onto each length of beading wire, sliding beads over wire tails. Slide a 3-hole spacer bar over all three beading wires.

4) Repeat step 3 five times.

5) Slide five 4mm beads onto each beading wire.

6) Slide a crimp bead onto one beading wire. Pass wire through corresponding loop on 3-loop side of second 3-to-1 link. Pass wire back through crimp bead and three 4mm beads. Adjust spacers so that they are parallel. Leave enough space between beads for bracelet to

be able to curve around wrist comfortably. Crimp the crimp bead. Repeat for remaining lengths of beading wire. Trim excess wire.

7) Repeat step 2.

8) Open five jump rings and connect all five together creating a jump-ring chain. Close jump rings. Open end jump ring and slide onto loop on one 3-to-1 link; close ring.

9) Open a jump ring; slide lobster-claw clasp and a second jump ring onto first ring. Close ring. Open second jump ring and attach it to loop on opposite 3-to-1 link; close ring. ●

Sources: *Mirror beads from Cousin Corp. of America; 3-hole spacer bars, 3-to-1 links and oval jump rings from Artbeads.com; beading wire from Beadalon; lobster-claw clasp and crimp covers from Fire Mountain Gems and Beads.*

MATERIALS

- 105 (4mm) faceted mirror glass round beads
- 6 (15 x 10mm) antique silver braided 3-hole spacer bars
- 2 (15 x 4mm) antique silver braided 3-to-1 links
- 6 (1.3mm) gunmetal crimp beads
- 6 (4mm) antiqued silver-plated brass crimp covers (optional)
- 6–8 (6mm) gunmetal oval jump rings
- 14 x 8mm gunmetal lobster-claw clasp
- 3 (10-inch) lengths .018-inch-diameter black nylon-coated flexible beading wire
- 2 pairs of chain-nose pliers
- Crimping pliers
- Flush cutters
- Tape

FINISHED SIZE
8 inches (including clasp)

Classical Floral
Dream

intermediate

1) Gently bend filigree oval over your wrist.

2) Slide jump ring onto end link of a 2-inch length of chain and onto open space at end of bent filigree oval; close ring.

3) In the same manner, use a jump ring to attach a second 2-inch length of chain to open space next to chain already attached; close ring (Photo 1).

Photo 1

4) Open a jump ring and slide it onto one half of clasp; thread jump ring through remaining ends of chains attached to bent filigree oval. Close ring.

5) Repeat steps 2–4 on other side of filigree oval.

6) Slide a jump ring onto end link of a 2⅞-inch length of chain; thread jump ring through same area where jump ring from step 2 is attached. Close jump ring.

7) Referring to photo and in the same manner, attach remaining end of 2⅞-inch chain to opposite end of filigree oval.

8) In the same manner, attach second 2⅞-inch length of chain to opposite side of filigree oval.

9) Using four jump rings on each side of filigree oval, attach chain links from steps 6–8 to top and bottom edges of filigree oval as shown.

10) Slide a glass bead onto a head pin. Form a simple loop above bead. Repeat 23 times for a total of 24 dangles.

11) Attach dangles to chains as shown by opening and closing simple loops. ●

Sources: *Stamped filigree oval, chain and jump rings from Michaels Stores Inc.; head pins and fire-polished glass beads from Artbeads.com.*

MATERIALS

76 x 32mm antique silver stamped filigree oval

24 (6mm) fuchsia AB faceted round fire-polished glass beads

18 (4mm) antique silver jump rings (opened)

24 (2-inch) 20-gauge black brass head pins

6mm antique silver leaf chain: 4 (2-inch) lengths, 2 (2⅞-inch) lengths

Antique silver toggle clasp

Round-nose pliers

2 pairs of chain-nose pliers

Flush cutters

FINISHED SIZE

7½ inches (including clasp)

Summer Day Charm

Queen Victoria popularized the wearing of charm bracelets as jewelry. Previously, they were worn as amulets to protect against accidents or diseases. She designed charms and gave them as gifts. Prince Albert gave Queen Victoria a charm bracelet for the birth of their first child and added charms for each of their nine children.

easy

1) String turtle bead, head first, onto a head pin. Form a simple loop, creating a turtle dangle.

2) String four bronze beads and dragonfly wings bead on a head pin. Form a simple loop, creating a dragonfly dangle.

3) String bicone crystal, bell flower and bronze bead onto a head pin. Form a simple loop, creating a flower dangle. Repeat with remaining bell flowers, for a total of eight flower dangles.

4) Slide a glass leaf onto an eye pin; center leaf on pin. Bend wire end with loop up positioning it so loop is centered above leaf. Wrap opposite wire end upward so it crosses just below loop. Trim wire end as shown (Photo 1). This creates a leaf charm. Repeat for remaining leaves, for a total of 15 glass leaf charms.

5) Slide one half of clasp and one end of chain onto a jump ring; close jump ring. Repeat to attach remaining half of clasp to opposite end of chain.

6) Lay chain out on a flat surface. Referring to photo and using jump rings, connect all charms and dangles to one side of the chain, keeping chain untwisted so all pieces are attached to same side. ***Note:*** *Do not use jump rings to attach glass leaf charms. To attach leaves, use round-nose pliers to open loop above leaf and slide it onto a chain link; close loop.* ●

Sources: *Antique gold charms, beads and clasp, Czech glass beads and CRYSTALLIZED™ - Swarovski Elements bicone crystals from Artbeads.com; chain from Blue Moon Beads; head pins and jump rings from Fire Mountain Gems and Beads.*

Photo 1

MATERIALS

Antique gold charms:
  2 star jasmine flowers,
  1 monarch butterfly,
  1 leap frog, 1 violet leaf
Antique gold beads:
  1 turtle, 1 dragonfly
  wings
12 x 8mm Czech glass
  medium leaves:
  8 wasabi luster,
  7 wasabi/olivine
6 x 9mm Czech glass small
  bell flowers: 3 metallic
  purple, 3 opaline light
  lavender, 2 fuchsia
8 (4mm) light amethyst
  CRYSTALLIZED™ -
  Swarovski Elements
  bicone crystals

12 (3mm) bronze Czech
  glass druk beads
6⅝ inches gold twisted
  cable chain
10 (2-inch) gold-plated
  head pins
15 (1¼-inch) gold-plated
  eye pins
17 (6mm) gold-plated
  jump rings (opened)
Antique gold 3-leaf toggle
  clasp set
Round-nose pliers
2 pairs of chain-nose pliers
Flush cutters

FINISHED SIZE
7½ inches (including clasp)

43

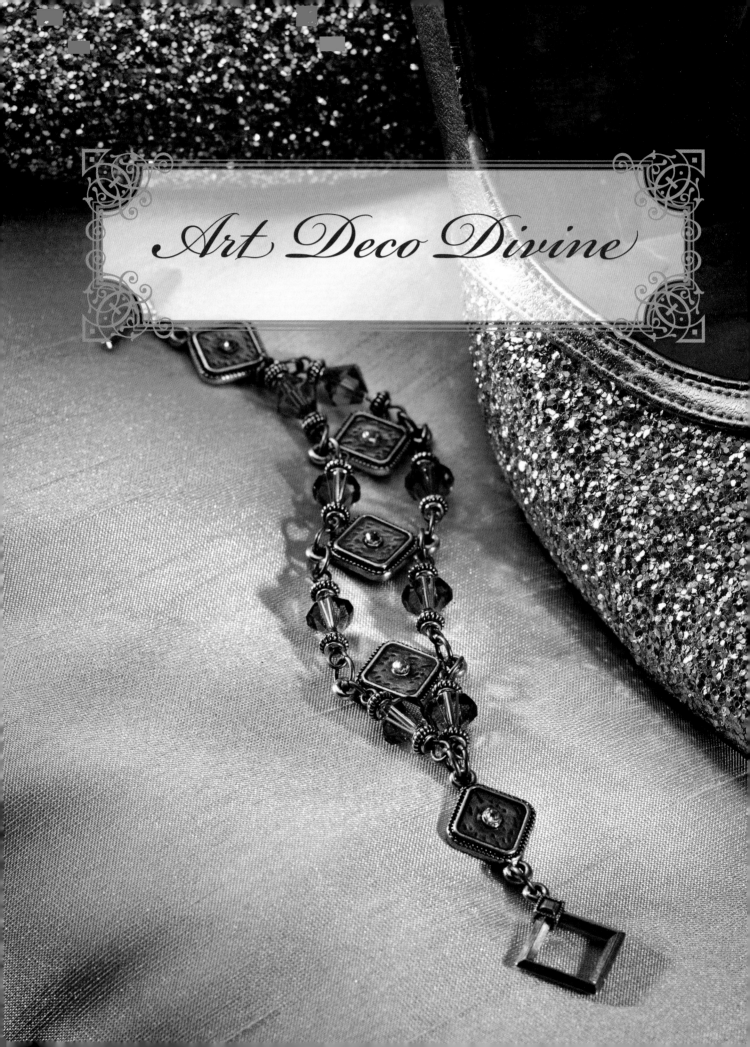

Art Deco Divine

intermediate

1) Slide a heishi spacer, bicone crystal and heishi spacer onto an eye pin. Form a simple loop above last heishi spacer, creating a crystal link. Repeat seven times, for a total of eight crystal links.

2) Use a jump ring to connect one half of clasp to an enamel link. Close jump ring.

3) Use jump rings to connect two crystal links to opposite side of enamel link from step 2. Close jump rings.

4) Referring to photo, use jump rings to connect ends of crystal links from step 3 to each end of a second enamel link. Close jump rings.

5) In the same manner, continue attaching crystal links and enamel links, referring to photo for placement, until there is one enamel link left.

6) Attach a jump ring to ends of both of the last two crystal links. Slide jump rings onto one loop of remaining enamel link; close jump rings.

7) Use a jump ring to connect opposite end of enamel link to remaining half of clasp. ●

Sources: *Enamel links from Cousin Corp. of America; CRYSTALLIZED™ - Swarovski Elements bicone crystals, heishi spacers, eye pins, jump rings and clasp from Artbeads.com.*

MATERIALS

5 (15 x 22mm) 2-loop green enamel links

8 (8mm) olivine CRYSTALLIZED™ - Swarovski Elements bicone crystals

16 (5mm) antique gold coiled heishi spacers

8 (2-inch) brass eye pins

18 (6mm) brass jump rings (opened)

Antique gold deco diamond toggle clasp

Round-nose pliers

2 pairs of chain-nose pliers

Flush cutters

FINISHED SIZE

7½ inches (including clasp)

Crystal Moonlight

intermediate

1) Slide a bead on a head pin. Form a wrapped loop, creating a dangle. ***Note:*** *Use first space in crimping pliers to press in end of wire on wrapped loop. Repeat for all head pins creating a total of 48 beaded dangles.*

2) Slide three different beaded dangles onto a jump ring; slide jump ring onto a small chain link. Close jump ring.

3) Repeat step 2 to attach all beaded dangles to chain.

4) Slide a jump ring onto one half of clasp and onto one end of chain. Close jump ring. Repeat to attach remaining half of clasp to opposite end of chain. ●

Sources: *CRYSTALLIZED™ - Swarovski Elements pearls, chain and head pins from Artbeads.com; Czech glass bead strands from Darice Inc.; toggle clasp from Blue Moon Beads.*

MATERIALS

8 (7mm) Tahitian-Look CRYSTALLIZED™ - Swarovski Elements round pearls
2 Smokey Silver Crystal Mix Czech Glass Bead Strands (#1999-M254)
48 (2-inch) black-finish pewter head pins
18 (6mm) gunmetal-plated jump rings (opened)
Toggle clasp with marcasite-style stones

6¾ inches gunmetal-plated oval link chain with large and small links
Round-nose pliers
2 pairs of chain-nose pliers
Crimping pliers
Flush cutters

FINISHED SIZE

8¼ inches (including clasp)

Green Isle
Romance

beginner

1) Slide a bicone crystal and rose gold bead onto a head pin. Form a simple loop, creating a beaded dangle.

2) Slide a malachite bead onto an eye pin. Form a simple loop above bead at a right angle to first loop, creating a beaded link. ***Note:*** *If loop is not at a right angle, grasp loop with chain-nose pliers and gently turn it into position.*

3) Open a loop on beaded dangle and slide it through bottom loop of filigree link. Close loop.

4) Open a loop on beaded link and attach it to top of filigree link. Close loop.

5) Open top loop of beaded link and slide it onto ear wire. Close loop. ***Note:*** *The filigree link has a front and back, so be sure to attach ear wire so front faces proper direction.*

6) Repeat steps 1–5 for second earring. ●

Sources: *Malachite beads and CRYSTALLIZED™ - Swarovski Elements bicone crystals from Fire Mountain Gems and Beads; rose gold beads, links, head pins and eye pins from Michaels Stores Inc.*

MATERIALS

2 (6mm) emerald CRYSTALLIZED™ - Swarovski Elements bicone crystals
Round beads: 2 (4mm) malachite, 2 (4mm) rose gold-plated
2 rose gold-plated filigree links
2 (35mm) rose gold-plated head pins
2 (35mm) rose gold-plated eye pins
2 rose gold-plated ball hook-style ear wires
Round-nose pliers
2 pairs of chain-nose pliers
Flush cutters

FINISHED SIZE

2¼ inches long

Rose gold is an alloy of copper and gold. The copper gives it the reddish color.

Tortoiseshell Dangles

●●○○
easy

1) Slide a bicone crystal, heishi spacer, rondelle, heishi spacer and a bicone crystal onto a head pin. Form a simple loop above last bead, creating a beaded dangle.

2) Form an ear wire from a head pin following the Turning a Head Pin Into an Ear Wire technique on page 12.

3) Open loop on beaded dangle and slide it onto small loop of ear wire. Close loop.

4) Repeat steps 1–3 for second earring. ●

Sources: *CRYSTALLIZED™ - Swarovski Elements bicone crystals and heishi spacers from Artbeads.com; fire-polished Czech glass rondelles from Jo-Ann Stores Inc.; brass ball-tipped head pins from Ornamentea.*

MATERIALS

4 (5mm) antique gold coiled heishi spacers

4 (6mm) mocca CRYSTALLIZED™ - Swarovski Elements bicone crystals

2 (9 x 6mm) gold/brown fire-polished Czech glass rondelles

4 (2-inch) brass ball-tipped head pins

Round pencil or wooden dowel

Round-nose pliers

Chain-nose pliers

Flush cutters

FINISHED SIZE

1⅝ inches long

Stones and organic elements like pearls or amber have long been thought to have certain mystical properties. Coral was thought to protect the wearer's health and was a common element in children's jewelry and baptismal gifts.

Champagne Drops

Queen Victoria was so sentimental that she had jewelry set with her children's baby teeth.

easy

Project note: *String bead caps so they "cup" the pearls.*

1) Determine top and bottom of flower link. Open a jump ring and connect it to bottom loop of flower link and to top link of a 1-inch length of chain; close jump ring.

2) Slide a pearl, bead cap and a bicone crystal onto a head pin. Form a simple loop above crystal, creating a pearl dangle. Repeat eight times for a total of nine dangles.

3) Open a loop on a pearl dangle and attach it to bottom link of chain from step 1; close loop.

4) In the same manner, attach seven pearl dangles to chain as shown alternating sides of chain. Attach last pearl dangle to jump ring below flower link.

5) Open loop on ear wire and attach to top loop of flower link; close loop.

6) Repeat steps 1–5 for second earring. ●

Sources: *Freshwater pearls from Cousin Corp. of America; CRYSTALLIZED™ - Swarovski Elements bicone crystals, jump rings, chain and ear wires from Artbeads. com; filigree bead caps from MK Beads; flower links from Kabela Design.*

MATERIALS
18 (5–6mm) champagne rice freshwater pearls
18 (3mm) crystal copper CRYSTALLIZED™ - Swarovski Elements bicone crystals
18 (7mm) antique copper filigree bead caps
2 antique copper flower links
18 (1½-inch) 23-gauge antique copper head pins
2 (6mm) antique copper jump rings
2 (1-inch) lengths antique copper cable chain
2 antique copper ear wires
Round-nose pliers
2 pairs of chain-nose pliers
Flush cutters

FINISHED SIZE
3 inches long

Cameo Silhouettes

beginner

1) Place a small puddle of jewelry glue onto a paper plate or plastic lid. Using a toothpick, apply glue onto oval inset of a filigree frame; place cameo onto frame. Let dry.

2) Open loop on chain tassel and attach it to center hole of oval frame along bottom edge. Close loop.

3) Slide a carnelian bead onto an eye pin. Form a simple loop above bead, creating a carnelian link. Using a jump ring, attach carnelian link to center top of oval frame; close jump ring.

4) Open top loop on carnelian link; attach it to loop on ear wire. Close loop.

5) Repeat steps 1–4 for second earring. ●

Sources: *Cameo cabochons and carnelian round beads from Artbeads.com; filigree oval frames and chain tassels from Laliberi; eye pins, jump rings and ear wires from VintageJewelrySupplies.com.*

Cameos underwent a revival of popularity in the 1850s. The finest cameos were carved from semiprecious gemstones such as onyx and banded agate. The stones needed to have a darker layer for the background with a lighter layer on top for the carved relief. Less expensive cameos were carved from shell, glass and lava from Pompeii. Popular carvings were Greek and Roman mythological figures and prominent historical personages.

MATERIALS
- 2 (13 x 18mm) white and peach resin cameo cabochons
- 2 (6mm) carnelian round beads
- 2 brass filigree oval frames
- 2 brass chain tassels
- 2 (2-inch) oxidized brass eye pins
- 2 (4mm) oxidized brass jump rings (opened)
- 2 oxidized brass small shell lever-back ear wires
- Paper plate or plastic lid
- Toothpick
- Round-nose pliers
- 2 pairs of chain-nose pliers
- Flush cutters
- Jewelry glue

FINISHED SIZE
4½ inches long

Antiqued Floral Brooch

intermediate

1) Referring to Tea-Dyeing technique on page 12, tea-dye bone marquise.

2) Referring to Creating a Beaded Circle technique on page 11, create a beaded circle using seed beads and beading thread. Adjust size of circle as needed to fit around flower cameo.

3) Use jewelry glue to adhere beaded circle to flower cameo by applying glue to edge of cameo with a toothpick. Let dry.

4) Apply glue to back of cameo and adhere to center of tea-dyed bone marquise.

5) Glue pin back to center back of bone marquise. ●

Sources: *Carved-bone marquise from Fire Mountain Gems and Beads; cameo, seed beads and beading thread from Artbeads.com.*

MATERIALS

63 x 32mm carved-bone marquise	10 inches silver Nymo size D beading thread
18 x 25mm black and ivory resin flower cameo	Beading needle
Approximately 36 (8/0) matte gunmetal round Toho seed beads	Toothpick
	Jewelry glue
¾-inch bar pin back	
	FINISHED SIZE
	2½ inches wide

Filigree
Flower Clips

easy

Project note: *The hinged clips can also be wired to the flower using short lengths of 24-gauge gold or black wire. If wiring clips to flowers, do so before beading clip.*

1) Trim shank from button with flush cutters. Glue button to center of star flower pendant. Let dry.

2) Referring to Creating a Beaded Circle technique on page 11, create a beaded circle using 12 (4mm) bicone crystals and beading thread. Slip circle of beads over button, adjusting size as needed. Bring ends of thread through to back of flower.

3) String bronze bead, 6mm bicone, bead cap (cup down), 4mm bicone and bronze bead onto a head pin. Form a simple loop above beads, creating a dangle. Repeat four times for a total of five dangles.

4) Use a toothpick to apply glue to loop of dangle; slide loop flat under beaded circle, placing dangle in the center of a petal of star flower. Repeat four times for this flower.

5) Glue ends of threads from step 2 to center back of pendant. Trim threads. Use toothpick and jewelry glue to secure beaded circle as needed.

6) Open hinged clip-on finding and determine placement on back of pendant. Glue to center of pendant. Let glue dry overnight before wearing.

7) Repeat steps 1–6 for second shoe clip. ●

Sources: *Star flower pendants from Laliberi; buttons from Jo-Ann Stores Inc.; hinged clips from A Costume Jewelry Shop; druk beads, head pins and needle from Artbeads.com; bead caps from VintageJewelrySupplies.com; bicone crystals from Michaels Stores Inc.*

MATERIALS

2 (50mm) brass star flower pendants
2 (½-inch) antique gold domed buttons
Jet glass bicone crystals: 34 (4mm), 10 (6mm)
20 (3mm) bronze druk beads
10 oxidized brass flower bead caps
10 (2-inch) antique brass head pins
2 hinged clips for shoe ornaments

2 (8-inch) lengths brown or black Nymo size D beading thread
Beading needle
Toothpicks
Round-nose pliers
Chain-nose pliers
Flush cutters
Jewelry glue

FINISHED SIZE
2 inches wide

Graceful Hairpins

easy

1) Using brown ink and referring to Dyeing Components With Alcohol Ink technique on pages 11 and 12, apply color to cabochons; let dry. Repeat using golden brown ink and a small paintbrush, dabbing ink into recesses of cabochons. Let dry.

2) Glue a cabochon to center of oval filigree hairpin; let dry.

3) Referring to Creating a Beaded Circle technique on page 11, use 35 seed beads to create a beaded circle. ***Note:*** *Check size of circle to see if it fits around cabochon closely and adjust size as needed.*

4) Apply glue around edge of cabochon using toothpick and slide beaded circle over cabochon.

5) Repeat steps 2–4 for second hairpin. ●

Sources: *Hairpins and flower cabochons from Laliberi; seed beads from Fire Mountain Gems and Beads; alcohol ink from Ranger Industries Inc.; beading thread from Darice Inc.; E-6000® jewelry glue from Michaels Stores Inc.*

MATERIALS
2 brass oval filigree hairpins
2 (8 x 13mm) ivory oval flower cabochons
75 (11/0) white pearlescent seed beads
Alcohol ink: brown, golden brown
White beading thread
Cotton swab
Toothpicks
Small paintbrush
Sewing needle
Jewelry glue

FINISHED SIZE
2½ inches long

Fancy
Filigree Pin

easy

Project notes: *If Etruscan swirl filigree is unavailable, try using a similar filigree piece. Slide bead caps so they "cup" the beads.*

1) Slide one end of a 2¼-inch length of chain onto a jump ring; attach jump ring to the second-to-last hole on one side of swirl filigree. Close jump ring. Repeat to attach second 2¼-inch chain length to opposite side of swirl filigree.

2) Slide both free ends of chains from step 1 onto another jump ring; slide jump ring through center bottom hole of swirl filigree. Close jump ring.

3) Place swirl filigree on a covered work surface. Stack Filigree Flower and Trillium Petals flower centered on top of swirl filigree. Using a toothpick to apply glue, adhere flowers in place. Add a dot of glue to center of stacked pieces and adhere a bead cap with points up.

4) In the same manner, adhere a bamboo coral bead inside bead cap; let dry. **Note:** *Make sure to position bamboo coral bead so that the hole of the bead will not show.*

5) Slide a coral bead, bead cap and filigree bead onto a head pin. Form a simple loop above last bead, creating a dangle. Repeat once for a total of two short dangles.

6) Slide a coral bead, bead cap, filigree bead, bead cap and coral bead onto a head pin. Form a simple loop above last bead, creating a long dangle.

7) Using a jump ring and referring to photo, attach a short dangle to each side and a long dangle to center of swirl filigree.

8) Paint back of pin back and any edges that will show through swirl filigree with brown paint; do not paint pin mechanism. Let dry. Glue pin back to center back of swirl filigree; let dry. ●

Sources: *Etruscan swirl filigree, brass flowers, filigree bead caps, filigree beads, head pins and chain from Vintaj Natural Brass Co.; bamboo coral beads and pin back from Michaels Stores Inc.*

MATERIALS

68 x 22mm brass Etruscan swirl filigree	Gold pin back
Brass flowers: 1 (20.5mm) Filigree Flower, 1 (15mm) Trillium Petals	2 (2¼-inch) lengths brass ladder chain
5 (7mm) brass filigree bead caps	Brown acrylic paint
Round beads: 5 (5mm) pink bamboo coral, 3 (7mm) brass filigree	Paintbrush
	Toothpicks
	Plastic lid or palette
	Round-nose pliers
3 (20-gauge) brass head pins	2 pairs of chain-nose pliers
6 (5mm) brass jump rings (opened)	Flush cutters
	Jewelry glue

FINISHED SIZE
2¾ inches wide

Buyer's Guide

Due to the ever-changing nature of the bead industry, it may be impossible to find the exact beads and components used in the designs shown in this publication. Similar beads and components may be found via the Internet or by visiting your local bead shops and shows.

A Costume Jewelry Shop
(432) 210-5968
www.acostumejewelryshop.com

A Grain of Sand
(704) 660-3125
www.agrainofsand.com

Artbeads.com
(866) 715-BEAD (2323)
www.artbeads.com

Beadalon
(866) 423-2325
www.beadalon.com

Blue Moon Beads
(800) 727-2727
www.creativityinc.com

Cousin Corp. of America
(800) 366-2687
www.cousin.com

Darice Inc.
(866) 432-7423
www.darice.com

EK Success
www.eksuccess.com

Fire Mountain Gems and Beads
(800) 423-2319
www.firemountaingems.com

iLoveToCreate™
(800) 438-6226
www.ilovetocreate.com

Imagine It Inc.
(845) 497-1026
www.imagineitinc.com

JHB International Inc.
(800) 525-9007
www.buttons.com

Jo-Ann Stores Inc.
(888) 739-4120
www.joann.com

Kabela Design
(610) 459-5816
www.kabeladesign.com

Laliberi
www.eksuccessbrands.com/laliberi/

Leisure Arts
(800) 526-5111
www.leisurearts.com

Making Memories
(800) 286-5263
www.makingmemories.com

Michaels Stores Inc.
(800) 642-4235
www.michaels.com

MK Beads
(239) 634-2232
www.mkbeads.com

Ornamentea
(919) 834-6260
www.ornamentea.com

Ranger Industries Inc.
(732) 389-3535
www.rangerink.com

Shipwreck Beads
(800) 950-4232
www.shipwreckbeads.com

VintageJewelrySupplies.com
www.VintageJewelrySupplies.com

Vintaj Natural Brass Co.
www.vintaj.com

The Buyer's Guide listings are provided as a service to our readers and should not be considered an endorsement from this publication.

EDITOR Brooke Smith

CREATIVE DIRECTOR Brad Snow

PUBLISHING SERVICES DIRECTOR Brenda Gallmeyer

GRAPHIC DESIGNER Nick Pierce

COPY EDITORS Rebecca Detwiler, Mary O'Donnell

TECHNICAL EDITOR Corene Painter

PHOTOGRAPHY SUPERVISOR Tammy Christian

PHOTO STYLISTS Tammy Leichty, Tammy Steiner

PHOTOGRAPHY Matthew Owen

PRODUCTION ARTIST SUPERVISOR Erin Brandt

PRODUCTION ARTIST Jessi Butler

PRODUCTION ASSISTANTS Marj Morgan, Judy Neuenschwander

978-1-59635-407-4   1 2 3 4 5 6 7 8 9